From,

Amy :S Swamper

Swamper

Swamper

Letters from a Louisiana Swamp Rabbit

Amy Griffin Ouchley

Louisiana State University Press   Baton Rouge

Published by Louisiana State University Press
Manufactured in Singapore
First printing

Designer: Laura Roubique Gleason
Typefaces: Vulpa text, Garton display
Printer and binder: Imago

Illustrations by Sandra Gay Brantley.
Photographs by Burg Ransom unless otherwise noted.

The author wants to express her heartfelt gratitude to Margaret Hart Lovecraft,
LSU Press editor, who believed in Swamper's talent from the beginning. She also
thanks her dear friend, Gay Brantley, who captured Swamper's personality with
her pen and brush.

Library of Congress Cataloging-in-Publication Data
Ouchley, Amy.
    Swamper : letters from a Louisiana swamp rabbit / Amy Griffin Ouchley.
        p. cm.
    Summary: Through a series of twelve letters, a swamp rabbit tells about himself
and his life in a northern Louisiana swamp. Each letter is followed by questions and
activities; Includes glossary and answer key.
    ISBN 978-0-8071-5074-0 (cloth : alk. paper) — ISBN 978-0-8071-5075-7
(pdf) — ISBN 978-0-8071-5076-4 (epub) — ISBN 978-0-8071-5077-1 (mobi)
1. Swamp rabbit—Juvenile fiction. [1. Swamp rabbit—Fiction. 2. Rabbits—Fiction.
3. Swamps—Fiction. 4. Swamp animals—Fiction. 5. Ecology—Fiction. 6. Letters—Fiction.] I. Title.
    PZ10.3.O855Sw 2013
    [E] —dc23
                                                    2012034247

For Hudson Christopher Ouchley

and

With thanks to my husband, Kelby, a loving partner on all adventures

Contents

Swamper

Introduction

My name is Amy, and I want to share an amazing story with you.

I am a naturalist and live in northern Louisiana near a type of swamp called a bottomland hardwood forest. One day I was leading a nature hike in the swamp with a group of students on a school field trip. We were using our senses of sight, hearing, smell, and touch to investigate the plants, soil, water, and animals in the environment. Suddenly a small brown animal darted out of a thicket ahead of us and started to nibble grass near the edge of the woods. We all froze so that we would not frighten it. I said in a whisper, "Let's watch."

I could see that it was a rabbit, but I was not sure what kind of rabbit. There are two kinds in the area: the eastern cottontail

Amy leads students on a hike in a bottomland hardwood forest environment. Photo courtesy of Bob Rickett.

A swamp rabbit has cinnamon-colored fur around its eyes.

rabbit and the swamp rabbit. They look similar, but there are some physical differences. I peered at the rabbit through my binoculars and saw that it seemed to be larger than an eastern cottontail rabbit and that it had cinnamon-colored fur around its eyes. The eastern cottontail rabbit has white fur around its eyes and is usually found in higher, drier areas. Swamp rabbits live in wetlands and do something eastern cottontail rabbits normally don't do: swim. I was sure that this was a swamp rabbit.

The students and I became curious and wanted to know more about swamp rabbits. Not long after our hike, I began to find letters in a hollow stump near my house. They were a bit muddy and a little soggy and were signed "Swamper." I could not wait to show them to the students. And now I want to share them with you, too.

This book contains the twelve letters from Swamper that I have found so far. They are filled with his adventures in the bottomland hardwood forest. To help you get the most out of Swamper's letters, I have added questions and an activity after each one; my answers are at the end of the book. And whenever you see a word that I made **boldface**, you can find its definition in the glossary I put together.

Have fun reading Swamper's letters. He and I both love our homes in the swamp!

Amy took this picture of Swamper's habitat in the bottomland hardwood forest while kayaking in the bayou.

Letter 1
The Web of Life in the Swamp

Swamper
Hollow Log
The Swamp

Dear Friends,

Welcome to the swamp. Let me introduce myself. My name is Swamper and I am a swamp rabbit. I live in a **bottomland hardwood forest**, which is a type of **swamp**. A long, lazy **bayou** flows near my home. Sometimes the bayou floods and spreads water all across the swamp. Then I and many other animals move to higher ground for a short time. This **wetland** is a superb place to find all the **resources** that I need: food, water, shelter, and plenty of space.

I have a variety of neighbors in my surroundings, or **environment.** Whisk, the white-footed mouse, is a **mammal** like me and lives in a grassy nest under my hollow log. I often see Whisk going about her daily activities. Silk, a golden silk orb-weaver, constructs her spider web in the branches over my log. I watch Silk work on her web and capture insects. A noisy Carolina wren named Cheer sings every morning in the bushes above my log. Blue, the great blue heron, flies over the swamp making loud squawks. Patches is a kind of turtle called a red-eared slider. He basks in the sunshine on a floating log in the bayou and then slides back into the water. Jug, the bullfrog, starts to bellow in late spring. His deep call, "Jug-a-rum, jug-a-rum," echoes across the bayou. The swamp provides a **habitat,** or arrangement of resources, for each of us.

There is a web of life here in the swamp. Silk's golden web reminds me how the plants, animals, and other **organisms** are connected to one another in this bottomland hardwood forest. One day I saw a butterfly trapped in the middle of Silk's sticky web. Silk was busy wrapping her strong webbing around the butterfly. I called to her, "Silk, what are you doing up there?" She replied, "I am saving this tasty butterfly for my next meal."

Silk is a **predator**. The butterfly trapped in her web is her **prey**. We all have to make a living in the swamp. Silk lives by trapping flying insects in her sticky web.

Butterflies play another role in the swamp. They and other insects help spread pollen between plants when they visit the flowers to sip their sweet nectar. Pollen helps the flowers produce seeds, which grow into more plants. This matters to me because plants are my main source of food. They give me the **energy** I need to live. The butterfly also gets energy from plants by sipping their nectar. Since Silk, the butterfly, and I consume food, we are called **consumers** in the food web. Plants are called **producers** because they make their own food using energy from the sun, water, and air.

Later that day I saw Silk eating the butterfly. "How does that energy taste, Silk?" I asked.

"Delicious," she replied.

Rabbits, spiders, butterflies, plants, and seeds all connect and interact in some way in this swamp **ecosystem.** The web of life in the swamp is as intricate and fascinating as Silk's web!

See ya later,

Swamper

Questions from Amy

1. What is the name of the type of ecosystem Swamper lives in?
2. What do you think is the ultimate source of energy for all the organisms in an ecosystem?
3. Why are plants called producers in the ecosystem?
4. Silk, the spider, eats insects. What is she called? What is the butterfly trapped in her web called?
5. Why are both the spider and the butterfly called consumers in the ecosystem?

The golden silk orb-weaver spider weaves a golden web as a trap for insects. Photo courtesy of Bob Rickett.

The red-eared slider is an aquatic turtle.

6

Wild roses grow near the edge of the swamp.

The question mark butterfly visits flowers for nectar.

The bullfrog makes a home in the swamp.

Activity

Think about how Swamper gets energy. Draw a simple **food chain** that includes: the sun (energy source), producers (plants), and several consumers (like rabbits, insects, spiders, fox, owl, alligator). Show each connection using arrows. The arrows must point in the direction that the energy is moving through the food web. Here is a simple food chain to get you started:

Sun → Plant → Butterfly → Spider

Letter 2
Swamper's Hollow Log

Swamper
Hollow Log
The Swamp

Dear Friends,

My hollow log makes an ideal shelter. Let me tell you about it. My log's story began with a fierce storm several seasons ago. I was living in a shallow hole in thick grass called a **form**. It stayed wet all the time. It wasn't the least bit cozy. A storm started one afternoon and raged all night. The wind whistled and howled in the treetops like a pack of coyotes. Endless rain poured from the sky. Sometime during the night I heard a loud crash, but I didn't know what it was. I was soaking wet and shivering by the end of the storm. All I wanted was a patch of warm sunshine.

I crept out of my damp form and headed toward the bank of the bayou. There lying in a patch of thick vines was the top of a hollow cypress tree. The wind had blown it down. I decided to take a closer look.

The log was about five feet long and narrow at one end. There was a jagged opening in the larger end. I entered the log through this opening and could see down the narrow, dark tunnel. A woodpecker hole about halfway down let in a bit of light. "This will make a perfect shelter," I thought. "It will protect me from rain, and these thick vines around it make good hiding places. It has plenty of space, and nearby are water and lots of plants for food—everything I need in my habitat."

I moved in and created a warm, dry nest for myself out of leaves and dried grass. For the first time in a long while I felt safe and secure.

Soon Whisk, the white-footed mouse, started digging her burrow under the log. That was fine by me. Whisk, which is short for whiskers, is a good neighbor.

Not long after that I began to hear scraping noises. I looked out and saw wood-boring beetles making a pile of sawdust. I did not like to see them chewing on my log, but I knew their work was part of nature's cycle in the swamp. These beetles eat some of the wood, and they also lay their eggs in the holes they make. The sawdust they make becomes a part of the soil and helps other plants to grow and thrive in the swamp. Nature doesn't waste anything but recycles nutrients, **minerals**, and water.

Many different kinds of insects work as **decomposer**s. Some other organisms that also break down natural materials are fungi and bacteria. They are neither plants nor animals. You can't see the bacteria because they are too small, but a beautiful assortment of mushrooms grows on top of my log. Mushrooms are fungi. Since fungi and bacteria can't use the sun's energy as green plants do, they must obtain their energy to grow and reproduce from the products of decomposition. They get some of that energy from my log!

The hollow cypress tree began to decompose long before my log home fell to the ground during the storm. Eventually my hollow log will decay completely and become what I call swamp fertilizer—a part of the soil of the forest floor. In the meantime, it is my home, sweet home.

See ya later,

Swamper

9

The swamp rabbit does not venture far from a hiding place.

A hollow log in the bottomland hardwood forest. Photo courtesy of Kelby Ouchley.

Questions from Amy

1. Why is a hollow log in a patch of thick vines in the swamp a good shelter for Swamper?

2. Decomposition is an important activity in the ecosystem. Give a simple definition of decomposition.

3. List the three kinds of decomposers that Swamper writes about in this letter.

4. What are some things that are recycled in nature?

5. What will happen to Swamper's hollow log in a few years?

Wood-boring beetles burrow into rotting wood.

White mushrooms, a type of fungi, are working to decompose this log.

Activity

Draw a picture of Swamper's hollow log in the swamp. Include a few decomposers like insects and mushrooms on it.

Letter 3
Swamper's Risky Role in the Food Web

Swamper
Hollow Log
The Swamp

Dear Friends,

Like it or not, I am a part of the **food web** in the swamp. As I mentioned in my first letter, my job or **niche** in the food web is consumer, specifically **primary consumer**. A primary consumer eats plants and is also called an **herbivore**. **Secondary consumers** eat primary consumers. They are called **carnivores.** I think you know what that means. Yes, that's right. I am the prey of a variety of predators around here. Foxes, owls, and alligators are some of the carnivores in the swamp that eat swamp rabbits. Thinking and writing about this risky business makes me nervous.

I eat green plants for energy to grow bigger, to reproduce, and especially to escape from predators. All primary consumers like me have to be on constant lookout for predators, who also need energy to survive. Running, creeping, jumping, hiding, and swimming are important survival skills for me. I have strong leg muscles and big hind feet that act like paddles in the water. To detect danger, I use my senses of sight, smell, and hearing. Being **wary** is one of my best talents. I call my skills and **adaptations** my "bag of tricks."

Yesterday evening I decided to grab a snack before resting in my hollow log. I poked my head out of the end of the log to survey the scene. Many other animals **forage** at this time of day. I know a red fox called Sly who makes regular rounds in the area. This is where things get risky, because Sly also is adapted to survive in this ecosystem. The rumor that foxes are smart and fast is true.

I have keen ears that can detect the slightest noise. So does Sly. I have a good sense of smell to sniff out the faintest odors. So does Sly. I have eyes on the side of my head that see what is happening on both sides of me.

His eyes face forward, but he also has good vision. I can run fast. So can Sly!

This evening I knew that I needed to take my whole bag of tricks with me to get that snack. And I was right. As soon as I started to **browse** on a few tender shoots of cane, I sensed that danger was near. The air was full of musky fox scent. My nose twitched when I smelled it.

Here we go, I thought. It's time to use some of my tricks. My first trick is freezing. My light brown fur has black streaks. I blend in well with the leaves and grass of the swamp. If I crouch and freeze, I seem to disappear into the background. I lay my ears back against my head, so this is called my "lay-low" position. This posture and **camouflage** protect me so that a predator can't see me. As I stayed motionless, I could see Sly looking around. Luckily the wind was blowing in my direction and not his. This prevented my scent from blowing toward Sly. His nose was up in the air and I could see that he was sniffing in every direction.

Suddenly the wind changed direction and he winded, or smelled, me. "Here he comes," I thought. It was time to use my next trick, called zigzag running. In zigzag running I dash and leap as fast as I can in different directions. I zip to the right, and then I zip to the left. Sometimes this confuses a predator and he loses my trail. I was hoping that this would happen to Sly, but I was disappointed. Sly kept coming, and he was getting closer. This was not good.

I was making a big circle toward one of my hideouts in thick vines, but I had to outwit Sly. Backtracking was the next trick in my bag. It is an excellent way to baffle predators. In backtracking I run back over my trail, usually on a log, and then jump to the opposite side. It's risky, but I was getting desperate. I needed to gain some time to get to my hideout. Sly quickly figured out my trick and kept coming after me.

It was time to head for the bayou, which was not far away. My plan was to jump in upstream and float downstream to an overhanging bank of the bayou. I ran to the water and dove in. Swimming is a life-saving adaptation in this swamp.

It worked! Fortunately, Sly is not fond of water. I stayed very still with only my eyes and nose above the water. I could see Sly looking down at the water and shaking his head. I knew what he was thinking: "We will meet again, Swamper. We will meet again."

I had outfoxed Sly one more time. Being a part of the food web in the swamp ecosystem is not always easy, but it's always exciting.

See ya later,

Swamper

Questions from Amy

1. An animal's role in the food web of the ecosystem is called a niche. What is Swamper's niche?

2. A primary consumer eats plants. A secondary consumer eats primary consumers. Can you guess what a **tertiary consumer** eats?

3. What do both Swamper and Sly need to survive?

4. Swamper said being wary is one of his best talents. What does the word *wary* mean?

5. List at least three adaptations that Swamper uses to escape Sly.

The red fox is a predator of the swamp rabbit.

A cane thicket.

Activity

Write another story about a narrow escape Swamper makes from a predator. Bobcats and alligators also prey upon rabbits.

Swamp rabbits browse on grass.

The bayou can be an escape route for a swamp rabbit.

The alligator is also a predator in the swamp. Photo courtesy of Bob Rickett.

Letter 4
Swamper Defends His Territory

Swamper
Hollow Log
The Swamp

Dear Friends,

I may look timid, but sometimes I must fight to defend my **territory** within the swamp. My territory provides just enough space and other resources for one male swamp rabbit, and that's me! I can understand why another male swamp rabbit would want to move into the area, but I don't need any more **competition**.

Near the edge of my territory is a cypress stump that makes a great lookout spot. From the stump, I survey my area. I also leave my scent on this stump. I have special scent glands under my chin that I can use for marking my territory. This behavior is called **chinning**. Swamp rabbits have a keen sense of smell, so other rabbits know that I live here.

Animals that are not rabbits may live near me because they do not use the same resources that I use. Cheer, the Carolina wren, occupies an old woodpecker cavity in the tree over my log. His loud call, "cheerily, cheerily, cheerily," announces to the other wrens in the area that this is his territory. Wrens live in pairs, so his mate, Wendy, resides here also. These wrens eat insects and spiders, which aren't on my menu.

There are several kinds of woodpeckers in the swamp, and they are always busy and noisy. The largest, the pileated woodpecker, hammers with his powerful bill on hollow cypress trees to signal that this is his territory. The drumming can be heard for long distances. He also uses his bill to peck and dig for insects like ants in big trees. Other woodpeckers with great names are the red-bellied woodpecker, yellow-bellied sapsucker, and hairy woodpecker. No, the hairy woodpecker is not hairy; small feathers on his legs and head only look like hair. Woodpeckers are good neighbors, because they don't eat what I eat. They occupy a different niche.

The other morning I was foraging for some succulent cane to eat. Have I mentioned that swamp rabbits have the nickname "cane cutter"? It was a fine fall morning, and fog wisps floated among the copper-colored cypress trees. Wood ducks were splashing and squealing out in the bayou, and I could see their ripples in the brown water. The ducks roost in a buttonbush thicket near my log. I could hear Cheer singing his wake-up call that I hear every morning just before the sun peeks over the horizon. Suddenly I caught the whiff of a new smell in the breeze, and I knew what it was. It was another male swamp rabbit.

Normally I try not to make much noise, but when there is an intruder in my territory I drum my hind feet on the ground with a loud "thump, thump, thump!" Now the other rabbit knew that he was not alone in this swamp.

Battles between swamp rabbits can be ferocious. Here is what happens. Both males stand on their hind feet face to face so that they can use their teeth and sharp claws. The rabbits will also jump up and strike out with the claws on their hind feet to hurt each other. Sometimes these assaults will result in serious wounds and cause the death of one of the opponents. My policy has always been to avoid a rabbit battle if at all possible.

So I took a precaution. To make sure that this other male rabbit knew this is my territory, I left extra scent markings around the edges of the area. This was my message: "Swamper lives here. No trespassing!"

I think he got the message, because I haven't found any more evidence of his presence. Many animals in the swamp defend their territories. Wrens sing, woodpeckers hammer, and I mark my territory with my scent. I can fight if I have to, but usually it's not necessary. That's a wise choice for us all, don't you think?

See ya later,

Swamper

Fall has come to the swamp.

Wood ducks roost, nest, forage, and raise young in the bottomland hardwood forest. Photo courtesy of Bob Rickett.

Questions from Amy

1. Why does Swamper defend his territory from other male swamp rabbits?

2. Swamper welcomes other animals into his territory if they are not male swamp rabbits. Name two other animals that have territories near Swamper's hollow log.

3. Swamp rabbits are also called "cane cutters." What does this nickname indicate about Swamper?

4. Why does Swamper try to prevent a fight with another swamp rabbit?

5. What two warnings does Swamper use to let the intruder know that he lives in this swamp?

The red-bellied woodpecker lives year-round in the swamp.

The male Carolina wren sings to proclaim his territory.

A swamp rabbit has a keen sense of smell that can detect another male rabbit nearby.

Activity

Resources in the eco-system are valuable to all the animals. Besides another swamp rabbit, what else could reduce the resources available to Swamper? Write your thoughts.

Letter 5
Swamper's Narrow Escape

Swamper
Hollow Log
The Swamp

Dear Friends,

"Caw, caw, caw." That is the call of the crows that fly over the swamp each day. These clever scavengers gather in the tall branches of an overcup oak tree over my hollow log and discuss their plans. At night they roost high in the tree. One day I heard them talking and arguing. "Let's go across the bayou and find something dead," squawked one crow. "No," said another one, "I want to go to the ditch beside the road. There is always something juicy there."

On and on they bickered. Yuck, I thought to myself, that does not sound appetizing. I think I will just stick to my tasty nibbles like grass and other green plants. I didn't know that a crow talking in his sleep would soon save my life.

I am **nocturnal**, which means I like to move about at night. Sometimes I am **crepuscular**, which means I will forage early in the morning or late in the afternoon just before dark. Nighttime is usually safest, because many of my enemies have a hard time spotting me. My brown and black-streaked fur serves as a camouflage in the dark swamp.

Last night I had a close call. In fact, I am just now feeling calm enough to write this letter. A great horned owl named Solo is one of the best hunters in the swamp.

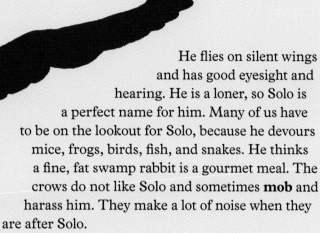

He flies on silent wings and has good eyesight and hearing. He is a loner, so Solo is a perfect name for him. Many of us have to be on the lookout for Solo, because he devours mice, frogs, birds, fish, and snakes. He thinks a fine, fat swamp rabbit is a gourmet meal. The crows do not like Solo and sometimes **mob** and harass him. They make a lot of noise when they are after Solo.

Events unfolded like this. It was dark with a glimmer of light from a crescent moon, and I was busy browsing on a patch of grass. I could hear a few crickets chirping around me. My dining spot was not far from the banks of the bayou. I heard a crow mutter, and I thought he was just grumbling in his sleep. Since the plant was so delectable, I did not pay attention. I should know better.

My ears are one of my best assets. They stand up tall and act like antennae capturing the faintest noise. Last night they worked overtime to save my skin.

I didn't know that Solo was perched high up in an overcup oak tree watching me. When he launched himself down at me, one of his sharp talons scraped the branch and made a faint scratching sound. Now I was sure that noise was a warning. I jumped off the bank into the inky black water of the bayou. I came up gasping for air and started swimming toward a thicket that I could barely see in the dim moonlight. A huge owl shadow swooped over me. I hid in the safe cover until I could creep back to my hollow log.

That narrow escape made me appreciate the crows in the swamp. Long may they grumble in their sleep and mob Solo, the great horned owl.

See ya later,

Swamper

A crow, a scavenger in the ecosystem, holds a snack in its beak.

Questions from Amy

1. Name at least two characteristics of great horned owls that make them good hunters.

2. Name any two organisms that great horned owls eat.

3. How are Solo, the great horned owl, and Silk, the golden orb-weaver spider, similar?

4. How do crows help clean up the environment?

5. The crows like to mob Solo. What does the word *mob* mean?

Ears for hearing help the swamp rabbit survive in its environment.

The great horned owl is a predator in the bottomland hardwood forest ecosystem. Photo courtesy of Charles Heck.

The rough green snake lives in the swamp.

Activity

Swamper's good sense of hearing helps him survive in the swamp. Think about how your ears help you survive in your environment. Make a list of some sounds that could mean danger to you.

Letter 6
Winter Comes to the Swamp

Swamper
Hollow Log
The Swamp

Dear Friends,

It is winter in the swamp. Days are short and cold nights are long. Winter happens in my swamp when its location in the **Northern Hemisphere** is tilted away from the sun. Some mornings the frosty Spanish moss hanging in the trees sparkles in the sunlight.

Here's some swamp trivia for you: Spanish moss is not a true moss but a flowering plant. It uses energy from the sun and minerals and moisture from the air to make its food. Tiny flowers bloom in early summer. Later in the summer, its wispy seeds float in the wind. They get trapped in the long gray strands of Spanish moss and then grow into new plants that make the moss even longer.

But back to winter. The cold air brings leaner times for me and the others in the swamp. All the animals work hard to find enough food at this time of year. After the trees have shed their leaves, they rest in the winter. I travel from my hollow log to search for cane and grass to eat. A good crop of nuts have ripened in the hickory trees. Many have fallen and bounced on my log with a loud "plop." A fox squirrel named Chat lives near me, and he uses sharp teeth to gnaw these hard nuts. Chat scampers and jumps in the oak and hickory trees near my hollow log. He pops his long bushy tail and chatters at me when I get near his nuts on the ground. I told him that I don't eat hickory nuts, but he didn't pay any attention to me. I hear Chat hard at work up in the trees gnawing the shells with sharp front teeth to get at the nutritious nut inside.

Whisk, the white-footed mouse, prefers acorns. I see Whisk hauling acorns to her nest beneath my log. Overcup oaks grow near my log, and one of their large, bumpy acorns will make a meal for Whisk.

A raccoon named Prowl fancies persimmons. White-tailed deer and opossums also dine on persimmons at this time of year. Big persimmon trees grow at the edge of the forest, and I noticed they are loaded with fruit. The persimmons taste best after a frost, and the other day I saw Prowl trekking toward the trees. I imagine that Prowl will stop along the way to dig for crawfish at the edge of the bayou. He is called an **omnivore** because he eats both plants and animals.

A few seeds and berries are still hidden on bushes and vines in the swamp. Many birds linger in the swamp to hunt for them. I hear the sounds of eating all around me. Animals of every description are chewing, gnawing, pecking, rooting, cracking, nibbling, and browsing. All of this talk about eating is making me hungry. When the sun begins to sink down the western horizon, I will venture out to find my secret patch of swamp cane.

The swamp contains enough resources for us all year long. I hope that you have enough resources in your habitat when the cold winter winds blow. Stay warm in your home, and I will too.

See ya later,

Swamper

Spanish moss is a flowering plant.

Questions from Amy

1. What causes winter in the Northern Hemisphere?

2. What kind of plant is Spanish moss?

3. What is the term for an animal that eats both plants and animals?

4. Give the names of three trees that provide food to the animals that live in the swamp.

5. Name two other animals that eat persimmons besides raccoons.

The raccoon is an omnivore. It likes to eat persimmons and crawfish.

A rare occurrence in the swamp: snow.

The crawfish defends itself by raising its pincers.

Activity

Find out how another animal—such as a white-tailed deer, black bear, or squirrel—survives in its habitat in the winter. Write five survival tips for the animal.

A fox squirrel chatters from its perch in a tree. Photo courtesy of Bob Rickett.

Letter 7
Swamper Moves to Higher Ground

Swamper
Hollow Log
The Swamp

Dear Friends,

At times my life gets complicated. Last winter was the perfect example. There was rain, lots of rain. Near my hollow log is a bayou that meanders through the swamp until it joins a big river. I learned from some songbirds, who travel farther than I do, that this big river runs into an even bigger river called the Mississippi River. The Mississippi River flows all the way down to the Gulf of Mexico. It's hard to believe that the water that flows by me every day is on its way to the sea.

When it rains, the water in the bayou rises. And when it rains a lot, the bayou overflows its banks and floods the surrounding swamp. This floodwater is called "backwater" in my part of the woods, and it dumps mineral-rich **sediments** onto the swamplands. Replenishment of the soil helps the plants grow, and that benefits all living things in the ecosystem, including me.

Many animals have adaptations to help them cope with the high water. Blue, the great blue heron, is a long-legged wading bird. Blue strolls around in the backwater gobbling up fish, frogs, and crawfish. Prowl, the raccoon, swims and climbs up in the trees to escape the floodwaters. I don't have long legs and have never been a tree climber. So I have to move to higher ground until the floodwater goes back down. Moving away from my home range is both interesting and dangerous.

Not far away from my territory is a special place in the swamp. It is called Pasaw Island. Old-timers used to say, "My pa saw a bear on the island in the flood of 1927." That's when it became "Pasaw Island." Many animals, including me, find refuge on this high place during a backwater flood. When surrounded by water, it becomes an island in the swamp.

Blue flies over the swamp on slow, graceful wings, so he knows what is happening on the far side. One day I asked Blue about the conditions. "Blue," I said, "how deep are the floodwaters?" Blue replied, "Three feet deep and rising."

The water was rising up to my hollow log, so I knew I'd better head to Pasaw Island if I wanted to survive.

When I got to the bayou, I saw Dawn, the white-tailed deer, swimming across. She was looking for a high place too. The current was swift and the water was black and rolling, but I jumped in and started to swim. Patches, the red-eared slider, stuck his head out of the water and said, "Keep swimming, Swamper, you've got a long way to go." Fortunately my legs are strong and I am a good swimmer. Prowl, the raccoon, was perched on a log snagged in a tree. That looked inviting, but I kept on swimming. I was hoping that I would not meet an alligator in the backwater. Alligators have been known to dine on swamp rabbits.

Soon I could see a hill of land surrounded by backwater. It was Pasaw Island and many different animals were there, but I did not see any bears. Also I had not encountered a hungry alligator on my trip. I had made it in good shape.

When I reached the island's edge, I climbed out and gave myself a good shake that sent water flying in all directions. Then I scratched my ear with my long hind foot. Wouldn't you know that my ear had started itching as soon as I began swimming? I was glad to be on land again. Next I had to find shelter and food and be on the lookout for owls and other predators. The owls gather in the vicinity of Pasaw Island during a flood, because they know there will be lots of easy pickings.

Luckily there was an oak log on the bank. I quickly dug out a form beneath it. After that chore was done, I went searching for food and found a good patch of greenbrier, a swamp vine. This would be a source of food for my stay.

If I was careful and used all my skills, I knew I could survive on Pasaw Island until the floodwaters went down. Then I would head back to my hollow log in the forest.

About a month later I came back to my home. The hollow log was damp but still there. I can travel when the flood comes, but I always like to get home again. Here's hoping I survive many more high waters.

See ya later,

Swamper

There are many egrets in the swamp. Long legs allow them to wade in shallow water. Photo courtesy of Mack Barham.

Swamp water floods the baldcypress knees.

The white-tailed deer must move to higher ground when the bottomland hardwood forest floods.

A great blue heron comes down to land. Photo courtesy of Mack Barham.

Activity

The flood changed Swamper's habitat for a short time. How might humans change Swamper's habitat for a long time? Write your thoughts.

Letter 8
Feathered Neighbors in the Swamp

Swamper
Hollow Log
The Swamp

Dear Friends,

I have many feathered neighbors whose habits and songs make the swamp a wonderful place to live. Some birds live in this swamp all year long. They are residents like me. Other birds come to the swamp to spend the winter but travel back north for the summer. Still others arrive in early spring after a long migration flight from the south. They nest and raise their young in this rich, productive ecosystem. These visitors depart in the fall to travel back to warmer areas for the winter. There are also birds that just pass through or over the swamp without lingering on their migration route in the fall and spring.

My neighbors Cheer and Wendy, the Carolina wrens, enjoy the good life in the swamp with me all year. I can hear them scratching and searching in the leaf litter around my hollow log as I write. Other bird residents include Blue, the great blue heron, several different woodpeckers, and Peter, the tufted titmouse. Gracie and Rufous, two small screech owls, also live in the area. I will tell you more about owls in another letter.

But now let me tell you about my friend Peter the tufted titmouse. He has a distinctive call that sounds like "peter, peter, peter." Peter eats seeds, which he will carry up to a branch and then crack open with his beak.

Peter is my resident watch-bird, because he warns me when there is a predator in the area. When Peter sees a large owl, such as a great horned owl, he hops around in excitement and scolds with a raspy "churr, churr, churr" call. When I hear this call, I stop what I am doing and look around to see what has bothered him. I have learned to heed his warnings.

A secretive visitor in the winter is the hermit thrush. This shy bird has a gray back and rust-colored tail feathers. His chest is white with dark spots. He is very handsome. I watch his behavior when he is perched on a branch near my hollow log. He cocks his tail up and then lowers it slowly. Another winter guest is the tiny winter wren, who scampers along the ground and hides beneath brush piles. I always enjoy these winter visitors.

Many kinds of birds fly over the swamp in the spring on their migration route north to nesting areas and in the fall back south to wintering areas. Some nights I can hear the geese talking as they make their way over the swamp. Other times I can see a large V-shaped flock flying across the moon-lit sky. I wonder about their long journeys. Where do they go? What do they see?

Swamp rabbits do not migrate, because we have adapted to living in a variety of swamp conditions. The only time I have to move is when the floodwaters rise, and then I find higher ground for a short stay. The swamp supplies my needs all year long, and that suits me just fine.

When spring arrives, the many songbirds return from their long trips and the swamp is filled with their calls. Ruby and Rowdy, the ruby-throated hummingbirds, come back from Mexico. Their travel stories are scary. They encounter high winds, cold air, and storms on their non-stop flight across the Gulf of Mexico. Somehow they endure these conditions and manage to reach the swamp to nest and raise their brood of baby humming-birds. Here, there are flowers with nectar and lots of insects to give them energy.

Last year I watched Ruby build her nest in the overcup oak tree. She gathered lichens, moss, and spider silk. The nest has to withstand storms that sweep across the swamp. The tiny cup-shaped nest looked fragile, but it did not fall down during a strong wind one night. Ruby's nest is a work of art, and I enjoyed watching her build it and raise her young. I like to see the hummingbirds return to the swamp.

These are just a few of my feathered neighbors. The swamp is the habitat for a wide variety of birds. They rest, forage, find mates, build nests, and rear their offspring using the resources in the swamp. This would be a dull and silent place without the birds. I hope my environment is always filled with many of these gifted creatures.

See ya later,

Swamper

33

The Carolina wren is a resident of the bottomland hardwood forest.

Questions from Amy

1. What's the word that describes birds that live in the swamp all year?

2. What's the word that describes the movement of the birds that travel long distances to summer or winter habitats?

3. Why don't swamp rabbits migrate?

4. Name two birds that migrate to southern swamps in the winter.

5. What large body of water must Ruby and Rowdy, the ruby-throated hummingbirds, cross to return to the swamp in the spring?

The usual call of the tufted titmouse sounds like "peter, peter, peter."

Birds migrate over the swamp in the fall and spring.

The ruby-throated hummingbird builds a nest out of lichens and spider webs. Photo courtesy of Bob Rickett.

Activity

Ruby's nest is built out of lichens, moss, fuzz from ferns, and spider silk. Gather some materials like string, grass, pine straw, twigs, and leaves. Construct a model of a bird's nest. Remember this: It's against the law to collect real bird nests. Besides, it could disturb their nesting.

Letter 9
Life Cycles in the Swamp

Swamper
Hollow Log
The Swamp

Dear Friends,

Every organism here in the swamp has a **life cycle**. It is born, grows, matures, reproduces, and eventually dies. If it is lucky, the organism makes it through every stage of its life cycle before it dies.

In a patch of sun near my log, there's a little oak tree that sprouted from an acorn last year. I've kept an eye on it and watched it grow a bit higher each month. All its leaves dropped off in the fall. When the floods came this winter and I had to swim to Pasaw Island, I worried that the young tree would not survive in the deep water. I checked as soon as I returned and it had made it.

Today I noticed its small buds were different. They had turned pale pink and were a bit larger. Later in the spring the little tree will have leaves again. Hopefully, it will grow and change for many seasons with the help of the sunlight, air, water, and soil. One day it will become a valuable part of the food web around here. It will supply many of my friends with its acorns and give me bark to nibble. I whispered to it, "Grow, little tree, grow."

Night before last I huddled in my log as buckets of rain fell and the wind shrieked in the treetops. There was a horrible, cracking groan and then a thundering crash. The next morning I peered out to find one of the giant oaks twisted and broken on the swamp floor. Its life cycle is almost over. Now it will decompose and nourish the other plants in the area, including the little oak tree. I thanked the big tree for all its gifts.

That evening I loped over to the bayou. Tiny lights began to flicker all over the swamp, and dozens of frogs called from the water. The flashing lights are made by little beetles I call fireflies. They have just emerged from underground chambers and are at the mature stage of their life cycle now. Their flashes are signals to attract a mate. The fireflies will die after about one month.

The frogs' calls are also signals to attract a mate. There are fast zipping sounds of the chorus frogs, the whistles of the spring peepers, and the chuckling of the leopard frogs. One frog starts calling, and soon others of the same kind join in the concert.

Jug, the bullfrog, popped his head up in the bayou. "How's the water tonight, Jug?" I asked him.

"It's finally starting to warm up, Swamper, and it sure feels good," he said.

Clean water makes a superb habitat for large **populations** of frogs. So all that frog music is good news to me and the other animals around here. We all need clean air and water.

I expect I'll soon see lots of frog eggs in the water on the edge of the bayou, and then a little later fat-bodied tadpoles swimming in the water weeds. I would not tell Jug this, but I know all the bullfrog tadpoles will not survive. Many will become part of the swamp's food web and be eaten by Blue, the great blue heron, other wading birds, turtles, snakes, and fish. Only a few will grow into adult bullfrogs like Jug.

I meandered down the bayou bank to see what else was happening. I met Prowl, the raccoon, along the way and he seemed to be in a hurry. "Where are you going?" I asked him.

"I can't talk now, Swamper," he replied. "I'm meeting someone special this evening."

I watched Prowl scamper down the shore of the bayou.

The air was filled with hints of fresh, new things. I sniffed a sweet aroma and glanced up. There was a crown of white flowers on a mayhaw tree. That was a welcome sight. We all wait for the fruit of the mayhaws to fall in May.

The year has cycled through its seasons of summer, fall, and winter. The life cycles of plants and animals continue, and many new ones are about to begin. Spring has arrived, and I am ready for it!

See ya later,

Swamper

Questions from Amy

1. Swamper writes about five stages of life. List them.
2. Do plants have a life cycle? Which plant does Swamper watch in the early stages of its life cycle?
3. What insect life cycle does Swamper see underway in the swamp?
4. Swamper experiences four seasons in the swamp. Name them.
5. How do frogs attract a mate? How do fireflies attract a mate?

A young oak tree.

Spring is a beautiful season in the swamp.

An old oak tree.

Activity

Swamper writes about some interesting organisms that he sees in the swamp. Become a nature investigator and find out about some other animal or plant life cycles in the swamp. Here are some ideas: bats, dragonflies, alligators, cypress trees. Write about your discoveries in the form of a letter like Swamper's.

Many tadpoles hatch, but few survive to become adult frogs.

A bronze frog, a common frog in the swamp, waits for a mate.

Letter 10
Swamp Moonlight

Swamper
Hollow Log
The Swamp

Dear Friends,

Mostly I am a loner. I spend nights finding food, eating, and hiding and escaping from predators. During the day I nestle in my hollow log and take it easy, though even at rest I am alert for danger. I have neighbors in the swamp, but as you know I don't like to socialize with other male rabbits. Female rabbits are another matter.

Once I dreamed of a beautiful rabbit. Her fur was golden and glossy. It glistened in the moonlight. Her ears were long, soft, and silky. Her eyes sparkled. She moved with graceful leaps by the edge of the bayou. When she sat up, she groomed her long ears in a slow, gentle motion with her front paws. As I began to hop toward her, I woke up and she was gone.

Ever since that dream I am more aware of the moon. I spend time out in the swamp during all its phases. It takes about one month to go from full moon to full moon. Let me tell you about it.

I'll start with the waxing crescent moon. It is a small sliver of light and does not stay long in the night sky before it sets below the western horizon. "Waxing" means it appears to get larger each night. This crescent moon waxes until it becomes a first quarter moon. A first quarter moon looks like one half of a white mushroom cap. Then it becomes a waxing gibbous moon, with a hump on one side. Every night the lighted surface of the moon increases and the moon lingers longer in the swamp. Finally the full moon arrives.

The full moon is a huge yellow orb when it rises in the east just as the sun is setting in the west. As the moon climbs up the sky, the swamp becomes luminous and magical. The swamp trees glow in the moonlight and cast long shadows across the floor of the forest. The full moon illuminates the swamp all night. As morning approaches, it descends down the sky to the western horizon. The full moon goes down below the trees just as the sun is rising in the east.

In its next phases, the moon appears to shrink, or wane, each night. First it is a waning gibbous moon with the hump now on the opposite side. The moon's lighted surface continues to decrease until it becomes the last quarter moon. After that it becomes a waning crescent moon and appears in the eastern sky just before daybreak. As it captures the light of the rising sun it looks like a sliver of pure gold.

Finally, the moon seems to disappear completely, but it's really still there. This phase is called the new moon, and the sun is shining on the moon's back side that I can't see. The swamp is very dark the night of the new moon. I don't see it again for a few days. Then late one evening I look up, and there is a thin arc of light just at dusk. It is a waxing crescent moon, and the phases begin all over again.

The moon was full last night, and I was munching on some sweet cane when I spotted another rabbit on the bank of the bayou. I sniffed the air and sensed it was a female swamp rabbit. She was browsing on some short shrubs. I watched her. Every now and then she would stand up on her hind legs to reach some tender shoots above her.

It is summer now in the swamp, a perfect time for a swamp rabbit to find a mate. The temperature is warm, and there is plenty of food. This female rabbit was long and sleek. I knew she would be a good mate for me.

I slowly hopped over in her direction. I did not want to frighten her away. As I approached, I made a soft noise. She looked up at me. Our noses touched and we began running, leaping, and chasing each other.

I told her my name was Swamper and learned that her name was Fern. I knew I had found the rabbit of my dream.

See ya later,

Swamper

The full moon illuminates the swamp all night long.

Questions from Amy

1. At what time of year does Swamper's letter take place?

2. Why is this a good time for swamp rabbits to find a mate?

3. When the moon appears to increase in size, what is it called?

4. When the moon appears to decrease in size, what is it called?

5. Where is the sun when a full moon rises in the east?

Swamp rabbits forage at night.

A golden full moon rises in the east.

Activity

Draw the phases of the moon in this order: new moon, waxing crescent moon, first quarter moon, full moon, last quarter moon, waning crescent moon, new moon. Be sure to label each phase.

Letter 11
Swamper and Fern's Offspring

Swamper
Hollow Log
The Swamp

Dear Friends,

The following notes are about my new offspring.

Day 1

I am happy to report that I am now the proud father of Lichen, a female swamp rabbit, and Moss, a male swamp rabbit. Fern gave birth to the little ones today. The babies are born hairless and will not open their eyes for four to seven more days, but they are happy and healthy.

Fern built her nest in a thick patch of coarse grass. She pulled the stems of the grass over to create a warm, protected den. Then she lined the nest with soft fur from her belly. I peeked inside the nest, and it looked like a good place for baby rabbits.

Male swamp rabbits do not help with the raising of the young, so I will stay out of Fern's way. She will spend lots of time out foraging and eating, because it takes lots of energy to nourish the babies. As a mammal, Fern nurses Lichen and Moss with her milk.

Lichen and Moss will stay in the den for about fourteen days and then they will come out to learn about the world. I can't wait.

Day 15

Lichen and Moss took their first look at the swamp today. Their noses twitched as they sniffed swamp mud and swamp grass. Their little brown ears stood up to listen to the swamp sounds. The crows were cawing, and Cheer the Carolina wren was singing his heart out, "cheerily, cheerily, cheerily." Lichen and Moss looked all around with tiny black eyes. They peered out into the wide world and then scurried back into the den. Maybe tomorrow they will be braver.

Day 16

Today Lichen and Moss ventured farther away from their nest. I tagged along to watch for trouble. Fern assured me that they have all the instinctive survival skills that we gave to them. *Instinctive* was a new word for me, but it means naturally in-born and automatic. Since Fern is their mother and I am their father, I bet they will be smart swamp rabbits.

Lichen and Moss bounded to the edge of the bayou. Moss did not realize that the muddy banks can be slippery and he slid down into the water. I watched his head go under and started to get worried, but soon it bobbed back up. He quickly paddled to the shore and climbed out. "Well," I thought, "it looks like he can swim." I noticed later that Moss instantly froze in a lay-low position when a hawk flew over, so that must be another of those instinctive skills.

Lichen decided she was going to eat an acorn. She chewed and she chewed and she chewed. She didn't have any luck getting into it. Swamp rabbits don't have teeth like Chat, the fox squirrel. Lichen then saw Moss nibbling on tender cane shoots. She discovered the cane was delicious.

Lichen and Moss have many lessons ahead of them. They will learn that life in this bottomland hardwood forest is not easy for swamp rabbits. If they are careful and observant, and use their instincts, they will begin to understand how this ecosystem works. They will survive the challenges of the swamp by using their bag of tricks just as I have.

See ya later,

Swamper

Questions from Amy

1. Do Lichen and Moss leave the nest immediately after they are born?

2. How many days pass before they open their eyes?

3. How old are Lichen and Moss when they go out to explore the swamp?

4. According to Fern, Lichen's and Moss's survival skills are "instinctive." What does this word mean?

5. Is swimming an instinctive skill in swamp rabbits? How do you know?

A juvenile red-tailed hawk eyes the ground below.

Swamp rabbits are born to swim!

A baby rabbit's point of view looking up in the bottomland hardwood forest.

Overcup oak acorns are squirrel and mouse food, not rabbit food.

Activity

Imagine other adventures that young swamp rabbits like Lichen and Moss might have in the swamp to learn how to survive. Write a short story of two or three paragraphs about those adventures.

Letter 12
The Owls in the Swamp

Swamper
Hollow Log
The Swamp

Dear Friends,

Owls play an important role in the swamp. Since they are one of the top predators around here, they help limit the numbers of prey animals such as squirrels and mice in the area. That keeps things in balance so there are enough resources for all the remaining primary consumers (herbivores), like me.

I have written to you about a close call I had with Solo, the great horned owl. There have been other times when I was almost an owl's meal, and that's why I stay alert. My running and swimming skills have been lifesavers for me many times, since owls and I are both active at night.

When an owl flies across the swamp moving its wings up and down in the air, the feathers do not make any sound. Owl feathers must be very special, because I can't hear an owl coming unless another animal warns me. I have seen the owls preening their feathers early in the morning mist high up in the oak trees. They use their beaks to preen, and this activity keeps the feathers ready for flight. All owls have sharp talons at the end of their strong toes. They swoop down and grab their prey with these sharp hooks. There is not much chance of escape from the grip of an owl. Their silent flight, excellent eyesight, and keen hearing make them first-class hunters. They are very dangerous.

The most common owl in the swamp, the barred owl, has bars across the upper chest and dark streaks down the whitish feath-ers of his belly. He has serious, deep eyes that peer around the swamp as he rotates his head from left to right. The most fan-tastic thing about this owl is the call that

echoes across the swamp, "who cooks for you, who cooks for you allllllll." Many times another owl will answer from across the swamp. Sometimes they banter in wild owl talk by hooting and hollering. Barred owls normally eat rats and mice, so they are not much of a threat to me.

The two small screech owls, Gracie and Rufous, nest in a cavity in one of the cypress trees. Rufous has reddish feathers, and Gracie has grayish feathers. On foggy nights they make a quavering call that pervades the swamp. This sound does not frighten me, because screech owls eat mostly insects and animals much smaller than me. They will catch and eat mice if they can, so Whisk, the white-footed mouse, has to watch for these predators. Screech owls don't like snakes and become very agitated if a black rat snake ventures into our area. This is helpful, because none of the rest of us is fond of this predator either.

The largest owls in the swamp are the great horned owls. These owls do not have real horns, but tufts of pointed feathers on top of their head. Their eyes are large and yellow, and it's best to avoid their intense gaze that means they have spotted you. The great horned owl's call is a soft, low "who, who, whooooo, who, who, whooooo." That's why they are sometimes called "hoot owls." When Solo hoots, the whole forest pays attention because many of us are potential prey.

Now while I am young and healthy I will use my skills, my speed, and my sharp senses to survive. Someday when I get older and slower, my own life cycle will end. I may become the prey of the owl or the fox. Those foolish crows will laugh over my bones. They won't have the last laugh, though, because one of my descendants will look up into the trees and chuckle when they see those hilarious birds. For now, I plan to enjoy life in the swamp for many seasons to come.

See ya later,

Swamper

A female screech owl. Photo courtesy of Bob Rickett.

Questions from Amy

1. Why are owls an important part of the ecosystem of the swamp?
2. Swamp rabbits and owls are active at night. What is the word for this?
3. Name three kinds of owls that live in the swamp.
4. What is preening?
5. Why are great horned owls called "hoot owls"?

A barred owl. Photo courtesy of Charles Heck.

A great horned owl. Photo courtesy of Bob Rickett.

Activity

Find out more about owls. Why don't the wings make any noise when an owl flies? What other animals are the prey of owls? Can owls or other birds of prey live in urban areas? Write down what you discover.

The sun sets on another day in the swamp.

P.S. from Amy

Swamper's letters taught the students and me so much about his life in the bottomland hardwood forest. Below is some more information that we learned through research. Find out if there is a bottomland hardwood forest near you and try to visit it. There may be a swamp rabbit living there. Whatever natural environment you inhabit, take time to use your senses and explore!

More about Bottomland Hardwood Forests

Bottomland hardwood forests are found not only in Louisiana but also along waterways from East Texas to Florida, in states along the Mississippi River, and up the East Coast.

Baldcypress trees in the bottomland hardwood forest.

They are bottomlands because they are low in elevation. They are hardwood forests because the most common trees are **deciduous** hardwoods. Deciduous plants shed their leaves once per year and remain leafless for weeks or months. Hardwood trees, like oaks and hickories, have broad leaves. Although the baldcypress, Louisiana's state tree, is not a hardwood, it is deciduous and also grows in bottomland hardwood forests.

During rainy periods, rivers, bayous, and streams overflow their banks and flood the surrounding low, flat areas. These low, flat areas are called **floodplains.** In Louisiana, wet periods typically occur in late fall and winter. During dry periods, the water in the floodplains flows back into the waterways or gets trapped in low areas. Bottomland hardwood forest can be found in these low, wet areas.

Bottomland hardwood forests are sometimes called forested wetlands or overflow swamps. They provide a habitat for many kinds of plants, animals, and other organisms that are adapted to their special conditions. This variety of life is called **biodiversity**.

Humans have changed many ecosystems, including bottomland hardwood forests. For example, in some places humans have built levees along the rivers, bayous, and streams. As a result, the water can't overflow and flood the bottomland hardwood forest. Since flood-waters are an important source of minerals, the bottomland habitat suffers. In addition, humans have sometimes drained and cleared the bottomland hardwood forests to grow crops and build structures. The ivory-billed woodpecker, a beautiful large bird, lost much of its habitat because of intense logging in southern bottomland hardwood forests. The ivory-bills could not adapt and have not been seen since around 1940.

Humans have also introduced plants and animals that do not belong in this ecosystem. If these introduced organisms grow and spread, they are called **invasive species.** Many times the invasive species change the ecosystem by taking over the habitats of the **native** plants and animals. The Chinese tallow tree is an example of an aggressive and harmful invasive species in the bottomland hardwood forests. Its leaves alter the soil's chemistry where they fall, and many native wetland plants can no longer grow there as a result.

Bottomland hardwood forests and other types of wetlands are important and valuable to humans. They help prevent flooding in areas where people live by soaking up extra water during rainy weather. As water moves through the wetlands it is filtered and cleaned. This improves the quality of the water for everyone. These swampy areas are places to enjoy many kinds of outdoor activities that do not harm the environment, such as fishing, bird-watching, hiking, and canoeing.

More about Swamp Rabbits

Like all rabbits, swamp rabbits are generally known as *lagomorphs.* This term comes from their scientific classification. Order: Lagomorpha; Family: Leporidae. The swamp rabbit is the largest of the eight cottontail species found in North America. Its scientific name is *Sylvilagus aquaticus.* These words come from Latin and Greek. *Sylvilagus* translates as "wood hare," and *aquaticus* means "found in water." Swamp rabbits do not live in the water, of course, but as we have learned they sure like to be near water.

Swamp rabbits have a cottontail but are of a different species than eastern cottontail rabbits.

The average length of a swamp rabbit is about 20 inches (approximately 502 millimeters). Its weight can range from 3.6 to 5.8 pounds (1,646–2,668 grams). Predators, disease, and hunters keep most swamp rabbits from living to an old age. A high reproductive rate helps maintain the populations of swamp rabbits in their environments. The average number of offspring is 3 and females typically have 2 or 3 litters per year.

Swamp rabbits live in the bottomland hardwood forests of eastern Texas, eastern Oklahoma, Louisiana, Arkansas, Mississippi, and Alabama and in small areas of Missouri, Illinois, Indiana, Kentucky, Tennessee, Georgia, and South Carolina.

In 1979, President Jimmy Carter had a famous encounter with a swamp rabbit while fishing from a boat near his home in Plains, Georgia. According to President Carter, a rabbit being chased by hounds jumped in the water and swam toward his boat. The president used his boat paddle to splash water, and the rabbit swam toward the opposite bank and climbed out. Many people didn't believe the president's story because they didn't know rabbits could swim. After reading Swamper's letters, we know that swamp rabbits can and do swim.

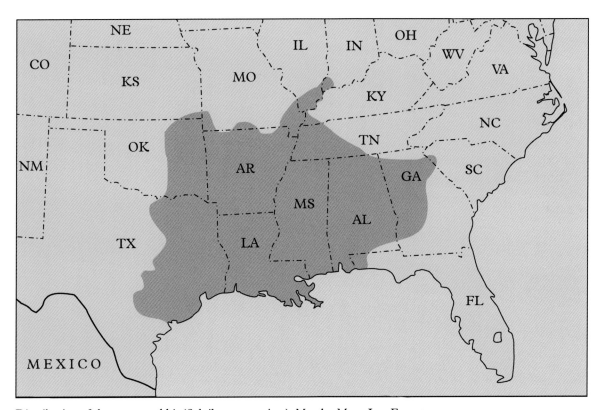

Distribution of the swamp rabbit (*Sylvilagus aquaticus*). Map by Mary Lee Eggart.

Answer Key

Letter 1
The Web of Life in the Swamp

1. Swamper lives in a bottomland hardwood forest, which is also called a swamp.
2. The energy in the swamp ecosystem and all other ecosystems comes from the sun.
3. Plants are called producers because they produce food by photosynthesis from the sun's energy, air, and water.
4. Silk, the spider, is a predator. The butterfly is her prey.
5. Both the butterfly and the spider are consumers because they consume food for energy.

Letter 2
Swamper's Hollow Log

1. A hollow log in the swamp is a good shelter for Swamper because food and water are nearby, it provides protection, and there is plenty of room inside it for Swamper.
2. Decomposition is to break down into simpler parts.
3. The three kinds of decomposers Swamper writes about are the insects, like the beetles, and fungi and bacteria.
4. Nature recycles nutrients, minerals, and water in the ecosystem.
5. Swamper's hollow log will decompose or decay in a few years.

Letter 3
Swamper's Risky Role in the Food Web

1. Swamper's niche in the food web of the swamp ecosystem is primary consumer, because he eats green plants.
2. A tertiary consumer eats secondary consumers. Here is an example of a tertiary consumer: Sly, the red fox, catches and eats a crow that dined on a dead mouse that ate a plant. Here is an example of a secondary consumer: Sly catches and eats a mouse that ate a plant. Sly can be a secondary or tertiary consumer depending on what he decides to eat.
3. Swamper and Sly both need energy to survive in the swamp.
4. The word *wary* means to be watchful and cautious.
5. Adaptations that Swamper uses to escape Sly are smelling, freezing, lying low, having camouflaged fur color, zigzag running, backtracking, and swimming.

Letter 4
Swamper Defends His Territory

1. Swamper defends his territory because there are only enough resources there for one male swamp rabbit.
2. Animals such as Carolina wrens and woodpeckers live in Swamper's territory. They have a different niche in the food

web and do not use the same resources as Swamper.

3. Swamper's nickname "cane cutter" indicates he regularly eats cane by cutting it off with his teeth.
4. Swamper tries to prevent combat with another swamp rabbit to keep from getting hurt or killed.
5. Swamper does two things: he drums his feet on the ground, and he leaves his scent by chinning the edge of his territory.

Letter 5
Swamper's Narrow Escape

1. Great horned owls are excellent hunters because they have good eyesight, good hearing, and sharp talons, and their wing feathers do not make any sound when they are flying.
2. Great horned owls are secondary or tertiary consumers that eat mice, squirrels, rabbits, frogs, snakes, and birds.
3. Both Silk the spider and Solo the great horned owl are predators. They are both consumers and carnivores in the ecosystem.
4. Crows help clean up the environment by scavenging dead animals and other garbage.
5. Many birds mob birds of prey like hawks and owls. The word *mob* means to chase, attack, or annoy.

Letter 6
Winter Comes to the Swamp

1. Winter happens in the Northern Hemisphere when that part of the earth is tilted away from the sun.
2. Spanish moss is a flowering plant.

3. A consumer that eats both plants and animals is called an omnivore.
4. Three trees that provide food in the swamp are persimmon trees, overcup oak trees, and hickory trees.
5. Opossums and white-tailed deer also eat persimmons.

Letter 7
Swamper Moves to Higher Ground

1. The bayou overflows and the swamp floods when there is lots of rain.
2. Swamper uses his ability to swim to Pasaw Island to survive the flood. His large hind feet make good paddles.
3. Swamper looks for shelter when he reaches Pasaw Island. Then he finds food.
4. Birds of prey and other predators find lots of food (prey) on Pasaw Island during a flood, because that is where many animals congregate.
5. Moving from his familiar home is dangerous for Swamper because there are lots of predators around and he has to discover new places to hide.

Letter 8
Feathered Neighbors in the Swamp

1. The word that describes birds that stay in the swamp all year is *resident*.
2. *Migration* is the term that means to travel long distances to summer or winter habitats.
3. Swamp rabbits do not migrate because they can find resources and shelter in the swamp all year long. They are adapted to survive the cold weather in their environment.
4. The hermit thrush and the winter wren

are two migrants that spend the winter in the swamp.

5. Ruby and Rowdy, the ruby-throated hummingbirds, travel across the Gulf of Mexico on their migration route.

Letter 9
Life Cycles in the Swamp

1. The five stages of life Swamper writes about are birth, growth, maturity, reproduction, and death.
2. Plants and all other living things have a life cycle. Swamper watches the early stages of the life cycle of the oak tree.
3. Swamper sees the life cycle of an insect called a firefly.
4. The four seasons are spring, summer, fall, and winter.
5. Frogs call to attract a mate. Fireflies flash their light to attract a mate.

Letter 10
Swamp Moonlight

1. Swamper's letter takes place in the summer.
2. The weather is warm and there is plenty of food. The female swamp rabbit will need lots of energy to supply food to her growing young rabbits.
3. When the moon appears to increase in size, it is called a *waxing* moon. The amount of lighted surface on the moon is what changes during the month. The actual size of the moon does not change.
4. When the moon appears to decrease in size, it is called a *waning* moon.
5. The sun is setting in the west when the full moon rises in the east.

Letter 11
Swamper and Fern's Offspring

1. No, baby rabbits do not leave the nest immediately after birth. Swamp rabbits are born hairless with their eyes closed.
2. Baby swamp rabbits open their eyes about five to eight days after birth.
3. The little rabbits are about two weeks old when they leave their nest to explore the swamp. They return to the nest until they are about three to four weeks old. Then the female rabbit will **wean** the young rabbits and they will leave the nest for good.
4. Instinctive skills are natural skills that rabbits and other organisms are born with and do not have to learn.
5. Yes, swimming is an instinctive skill in swamp rabbits, because Moss could swim the first time he entered the water.

Letter 12
The Owls in the Swamp

1. Owls are one of the top predators and help limit or control the numbers of prey animals like mice, rabbits, and squirrels. That helps keep enough resources such as plants, seeds, and nuts available for Swamper and other herbivores.
2. An animal that is active at night is *nocturnal.*
3. Three owls that live in the swamp are the barred owl, the screech owl, and the great horned owl.
4. Birds groom their feathers with their beaks. This behavior is called *preening.*
5. Great horned owls are called hoot owls because of their call, "who, who, whooooo."

Glossary

Adaptation: A feature or behavior that helps an organism survive in its environment.

Bayou: A slow-moving waterway that flows through swamps and other lowlands.

Biodiversity: A term used to represent the variety of life forms in a given area.

Bottomland hardwood forest: A forested wetland found in low areas along a river, bayou, or stream that may flood during rainy seasons.

Browse: To nibble or feed on leaves and shoots.

Camouflage: Protective coloring or markings that help an organism blend in with its surroundings (a physical adaptation).

Carnivore: A meat eater.

Chinning: The behavior of marking one's territory with a special scent from glands on the chin.

Competition: The demand at the same time by two or more organisms for limited resources, such as nutrients, living space, or light.

Consumer: An organism that eats producers and other organisms in the ecosystem.

Crepuscular: Active at dawn or dusk.

Deciduous tree: A tree that loses its leaves at the end of the growing season.

Decomposer: An organism that breaks down dead materials and returns the nutrients and minerals to the ecosystem.

Bacteria, fungi, and insects are all decomposers.

Ecosystem: The interactions between all the living and nonliving things in an environment.

Energy: The capacity to do work. Kinds of energy include light, sound, heat, electrical, chemical, and mechanical.

Environment: The living and nonliving surroundings of an organism.

Floodplain: The low-lying land near a stream, bayou, or river that is covered by water during times of heavy rainfall when water overflows the banks.

Food chain: A simple way to show the transfer of energy from one organism to the next in an ecosystem.

Food web: The connecting food chains in an ecosystem.

Forage: To search for food.

Form: A depression in the ground used as shelter by a rabbit.

Habitat: The arrangement of food, water, shelter, and space suitable to an animal's needs.

Herbivore: A plant eater.

Invasive species: An organism introduced into an ecosystem to which it doesn't belong, and which then grows and spreads, changing the ecosystem in potentially harmful ways.

Life cycle: The series of stages and changes that living things experience from birth to death.

Mammal: An animal with a backbone (**vertebrate**) that feeds its young with milk and has hair. Most mammals give birth to live young.

Migration: The regular movement of some animals from one region to another for feeding or breeding.

Mineral: A solid, naturally occurring substance that was not made by plants or animals. Many kinds of minerals such as calcium and nitrogen are needed for us to live a healthy life.

Mob: To chase, attack, or annoy.

Native: Originating in a certain region.

Niche: An organism's "job" or role in its ecosystem.

Nocturnal: Active at night.

Northern Hemisphere: The half of the earth north of the equator.

Omnivore: A consumer that eats both plants and animals.

Organism: Any living thing.

Population: All of the members of one species that live in a defined area.

Predator: An animal that hunts, kills, and eats other animals (prey).

Prey: An animal that is hunted, killed, and eaten by other animals (predators).

Primary consumer: An organism that feeds on producers (green plants).

Producer: An organism that makes its own food by photosynthesis, using energy from the sun plus carbon dioxide and water. Producers are a source of food (energy) for consumers.

Resource: Something necessary or useful to an organism, such as food, water, shelter, and space.

Secondary consumer: An organism that eats a primary consumer.

Sediment: Matter that settles to the bottom of a liquid, especially materials such as sand, soil, and gravel deposited by wind, water, and ice in bodies of water.

Swamp: A wetland with trees.

Territory: The area an animal defends to protect its resources.

Tertiary consumer: An organism that eats a secondary consumer.

Vertebrate: An animal with a backbone. This category includes amphibians, fish, birds, mammals, and reptiles.

Wary: Being very cautious and watchful.

Wean: To accustom a young mammal to take food other than by nursing.

Wetland: A landform characterized by the presence of water at some time during the year, hydric soils, and hydrophytic (water-loving) vegetation.

OUR RECEIPT
THANK YOU

8:10AM
0000#4386   CLERK

WELRY $2
OURS $2
SE ST $2
MY $

LENS   20
TOTAL $26
CASH $
HANGE